Racing Ravens

A Poetry Collection

C. Churchill

Also, by C. Churchill

Petals of the Moon

Wildflower Tea

I am a woman not a Winston

Instagram @cc_writes

Facebook @cc_writes

Racing Ravens

A Poetry Collection

C. Churchill

There is a saying that when you find a black feather it is the universe telling you that your angels are watching over you and that you are not alone.

A heart that has lived in another's will never beat the same again.

racing ravens
chasing pines

finally lost
finally found

among the birches
among the rains

tears shed fiercely
release this pain

for I am wildflower
to be reborn

after the flood
after the storm

-racing ravens

When we lose that soulmate, that one and only, that forever, we duck, we dive, we hide from love as if learning to love again will only bring us more pain.

But if we can breathe and take a moment to settle our pain, then we realize a soulmate would never want us to give up.

Especially, on love.

This collection is dedicated to widows everywhere, from one to another because we exist.

Racing Ravens is collection of poems written to inspire and help others feel not alone in their grief. I became a widow in the summer of 2006. My husband, best friend was murdered one night in a road rage incident. Grief is a strange beast and it so often feels like drowning, funny thing is the waves are intermittent and mostly invisible. One moment you are fine and the next crumpled in the middle of the floor holding a card you found hidden among old papers. Whatever the situation, it is real, it's heart wrenching and it needs to have a voice. Being a young widow has had several challenges that are unique. A loss is a loss and I feel this collection will not only connect with widows but anyone who has experienced great and tragic loss in their life.

*Every day I watched
what I know*

become what I knew

I didn't lose an arm
but I had phantom pain
the one they talk of
when you lose a limb
it was in my chest
my heart
still beating
or at least going through the
motions
I existed
but hollowed out
like an old oak tree
no longer growing
standing as still as can be
not a leaf, nor a bud
just dry, solid
and trying to stand tall
through echoes of
Once upon a time

-hollow

I didn't want a shower
I didn't want to wash my hands
I didn't want to leave your side but
they insisted I wash you from me
your blood from my skin
your hands from my hands
they told me I had to wash you off
of me and I held you tighter
and continued to tell you I love you
my hands and your blood were the
least of my worries
and the most

-it was everything

C. Churchill

They saw me bare
and handed me dead leaves

instead of embraces

-forgetting how we grow

These walls
once filled with laughter

these timbers
once filled with love

remembering the light dance
on frames of memories

now watching dust collect
over smiling faces

because I can't wipe them anymore
my hands have become busy

collecting tears and holding my
chest wishing you were here

knowing you are gone
knowing I may never dance again

-the moment a home becomes a cage

Blankets of night cover the sun
days turn to weeks
and months to years
one day there is snow
the next there is rain
all while I sit in your chair
coffee in hand
under a blanket of night

-blankets of night

All the want
all the need
all the hope
all the greed
nothing to say
nothing to do
nothing but sit
and think of you

-lost

There may have been a full moon
there may have been
a canopy of stars
I didn't see a firefly light
that summer night
I was standing in the dark
feeling my way through
something alien
looking for you in every corner
while explaining to our dogs
you were never coming home
I watched your good boy take his
post waiting for your arrival
as he did every evening
he sat at the door
as a good boy does
staring into the darkest night
we both knew
but we both searched
I crumpled when he whined
when he cried

when he realized
his post was no longer necessary

-the darkest night

After the parade left,
I sat in my forty acres
I looked out towards the sky
wondering what may become
of a life once tethered to him
tears had come and gone
friends had become awkward

I was dwelling now
spiraling in a pool

where the wind carried memories
and the view
hauntingly enormous

that is when my what may become
was answered by

anything I want

-strange freedoms

Grief has a timetable

That is no one's business

Yes I lost my mind
I have been there without words,
without breath
hearing the headline ringing in my
ears "he isn't going to make it" and
then the buzzing of too bright
fluorescent lights and too loud of
smiles
I needed a pause a moment to be
still because twelve hours ago all I
could see was you looking into my
eyes saying you were so glad you
married me
and the sun kissed our skin
while we rode the waves
and we had everything
we had ever wanted

-12 hours ago

The wind has no name
but it calls me all the same
the sun has no darkness
but all I see is shadow

Faces blurred
in the "how are you's"
and the "I am sorry's"
a constant patter
for a few sleeps, at least
or a few eyes wide
at the ceiling nights
eventually
the patter slowed
but my eyes couldn't stop staring
wondering
what the fuck was happening
I saw you die
I held your last breaths
in my arms
I saw the fucking flatline
I couldn't decide if I was crazy or
my reality just took
a very wrong turn
I was blurry, I was hurting
all I could muster
all I could say was "I am doing as
good as expected" and "Thank you"

because we fall into line
when everything else falls apart

-fuck as expected

I planted roses
I didn't want arrangements
I didn't want more death
I wanted hope
I needed hope
after the funeral
eighteen rose bushes were planted
I needed you to live
in a garden where I could feel life
amongst all the death

friends and family together
shared a moment
with smiles of memories
creating something new
we needed you to live on
in any capacity
as my eyes adjusted to my reality

I saw smiling
I saw laughing
I saw hope
under the walnut tree
among friends
I felt the warmth of sunshine

and I wondered if you could see
how much you were loved

because I needed you to know

I needed the roses
and smiles to reach you

and just as I was wondering
the tree we always sat under
released a nut that landed squarely
in the backside of my pants
something that would have made
you laugh,
a full belly laugh
and I smiled into the sky
knowing you were there

and would live on

-little things

Beware the raven with shiftless
eyes
beware the circle over deaths
demise
beware the scavengers
who pick you clean
beware the souls
who watch you scream

beware

beware

for this world is not as it seems
guises travel lightly,
and masks are far too common

beware, beware

-beware

Cardinals land just so
as if they already know

that you have a missing part
someone missing from your heart

Cardinals land just so

letting us know

letting us know

-landing

The sky opened

for the first time

in a long time

I saw hope

I felt sunrise

I felt imagination

unusual for a victim

at every moment of revelation

I was a whore

I was a noncompliant

I was not worthy of my loss

because I saw hope

-hope

How do you say goodbye?
how do you wake to an empty bed?
how do you continue
when things are suddenly
upside down
inside out
and ripped from the core
how do you trust gravity?
how do you trust anyone?

or anything?

you carry on
in all doubt
you carry on

doing whatever it takes
to get your ass out of bed
and if they don't agree

Fuck them.

because you decided to live

-fully

Keep that chin up
hike up your bootstraps
put on your big girl panties

mantras
must haves
words that I had to repeat
with every tear
that crossed my cheek
eyes welled
as fear swelled
how was I to do this?
this living thing?

how was I to start new
when a trip to the local grocer
caused whispers
small towns have large voices
with the echoes of murder
widow and sadness

mantras be damned,
they couldn't quiet the spectators

I had become everyone's
favorite crime scene
and I couldn't help but run

so, I ran

-a new life

Becoming a warrior doesn't happen overnight

but becoming a widow does

and as opposite as the two seem

they run parallel

Being lost
takes on a new meaning
when you disappear
when you choose to run
straight in the wild
and not look back
sometimes, we need
to chew off our own foot before
we can dance again

-all it takes is a brave moment

I drove away
from everything I knew
every memory
every pain

I was wild

I was free

I was

inexplicably me

-dwelling be damned

I carried my pain between
bark and splinter
not near enough to flame
I carried my tears in
a cloud of confusion
not near enough to quench
I carried your heart under my wing
not near enough to fly
I carried it
this mule of grief
winding down a mountainside

-not near enough

I ran for the shore
because water was my home
the one, I remember for my youth
my safe place
the place where waves lapped
where sun prismed
where the only sound
was my breath and life

but in a simple way
it was life on my scale

and breaks are necessary
when you are
drowning in air

 sometimes the water is safer

-overwhelmed

I couldn't describe what loss was
I had never been very good at that

my father lost his life
when I was very young
and I saw how I was supposed to
act they told me how
they told me I was wrong
I saw again
but still never managed
my grieving to their standards
because grieving

has its own time

-no matter what they say

I walk in the fern

as if they know my sadness

as if they grow to cover me

they curl over me

when no one else understands

the earth

takes my hand

and guides me to the reality

that we are here to breathe

we are here to care

we are here

to live

-learning

I learned to forgive those

who didn't understand

I watched the leaves drop
another season had gone
and just as the one before
I felt you
your tears on my cheek
your lips on my neck
your hand on my heart
holding it just as fiercely
as the day you

became the leaves

-seasons of you

I will never not see you
I will never forget your name
I will never hold anyone's hand
the way I held yours

-and that is perfectly fine

C. Churchill

My head lay on the concrete
as thoughts pooled around me,
I looked dead to many that passed
yet not one hand was given

my thoughts formed a river
bleeding into the gutter,
yet I held on watching my mind
turn pain into words and words
into verse
I held on
while others let me go only to
realize they didn't like poetry

-poetry

Have you seen the trees
out the corner of eyes?
a sideways blur
on a highway of lies
have you seen the sky
lighting up the night
filled with regret and a touch of
fright?
have you seen the rivers
how they flow
winding a tendril of things
we already know?
have you seen a heart
beating with velocity
while others see only an atrocity?

have you looked?
have you wondered?
have you thought they were blind?

when they cannot see past a simple
rhyme

-simpletons

I envy those who don't know
how long it took

for my heart to regrow

-invisible in grief

the harder they hit

the higher I flew

A wishing well lives
down the road
abandoned in life's problems
deterioration has taken toll
running it dry of aspirations
the only wish it wishes now
is a rain of hope
a flood of dreams

anything to bring back its purpose

-purpose

I let grief wash over me

time and time again

until I couldn't find the shore

until I assured myself

I couldn't be happy again

-sometimes we can't help it

Blisters weaken
hearts are worn
let me refrain from
thoughts unformed
the tears they wash
bitter chains
cutting deep
a slow death rain
hear my heart
stutter in beat
watch me fumble
these two left feet
find the night
the darkness lay
between two tears
always this pain
but alas
my heart
claims this scurry
no need to wince
no need to worry
this pain
keeps me wild

the moon
keeps me sane
and I carry the night
my slow death rain

-slow death rain

I wanted to scream
I was done with tears
I was done being thought of as a
broken mirror
collecting dust, waiting
for garbage day
unlucky as they come
that is what they say
I was done with their perceptions
they never stayed longer than a
song and they never saw
that my mirrored pieces
didn't really belong
I became a mosaic
a kaleidoscope of pain
I became everything through being
shattered
least of all sane

-work of art

denial
anger
bargaining
depression
acceptance
denial
anger
bargaining
depression
acceptance
denial
anger
bargaining
depression
acceptance
denial
anger
bargaining
depression
acceptance
denial
anger

-stages of grief

They may never know
that you laid with them
in that hospital bed
making every bargain
with every deity
questioning faith
but applying to all of them

they may never know
that tears can stop coming if you
don't drink enough water,
they may never know
that you stopped your breath
to find just one more

they may never know that standing
can be impossible
when your legs
no longer have purpose,
they may never know your grief

but you do
and you are still breathing
and still standing

-stand tall

Death became a worthy adversary
I remember that moment when I
didn't care if I was taken
I no longer had the usual fear
my compass now pointed
in a different direction
to grab every moment
and hold it dear
to watch the ravens circle
and appreciate their grace
to feel the wind on my skin
and not mind the cold
to sit in the blades of dew-covered
grass without a care
just feeling this life for all it is
and all it can be

death became a worthy adversary
when I no longer cared
when death took me

-truly living

When the rain gets in your bones
wishing you weren't so alone
remember
the sun will come again

warming

touching

smiling

again

-you got this

my dark quiet places

are filled with light

I am silent in slowing breath
taking notice of the linens

how the pillow is cased
forms to my face and cradles my
tears

how the covers find cover in my
darkness and the curtains sway
in the breeze of my thoughts

I am silent

as the darkness speaks

-silence

I sat with your t-shirt
packing up boxes
in a quiet room once filled with
laughter

I sat with your t-shirt
the one you painted when we were
young, and tie dyed

I sat with your t-shirt knowing
your hands created this design
with small bottles of paint
and brushes

I sat with your t-shirt
remembering your hands

and I couldn't

put you in a box

-remembering your touch

It will hit you hard as bricks
out of the blue
it could be a song
in the middle of a department store
it could be
a silly Christmas ornament
it could be anything
at any time
and in those moments
I used to fear
I now embrace the fact
that at one time

you were here

-and I smile

Some days
I want them to see my heart

how it has been
bloodied and ripped apart

and some days

I want to pretend I haven't lost
the only person that made me feel
alive

-all about balance

I was bred to be a warrior
I had no choice
watching my father
work to the bone
watching him die
before my young eyes
when he passed
I watched a widow mother
try to survive
making sense when there is
none in tragedy
then suffering the same fate
widow life is hard
it is unexpected
it is the twilight zone
but warriors live on fighting
for love in all the right places

don't let them tell you different

-widows are warriors

Who do you seek
in the darkness of night?
hand outstretched grasping
the cold pillow next to you
what do you feel in the rain?
longing for a kiss long lost
what do you see in the future
mirror?
a sting of past reflection

may your woes and worries
transcend to peace and hope
for the yesterdays
are blurry in distance
your future lies in a clear tomorrow
energy moves forward
only halted by regret and sorrow

-move forward

Blooms in darkness

petals of black

fall silent

victims of life

a shadow embraces

erases time

plucked in envious discard

we wait for the sun

-hiding

Don't let others

play you into their pain

you are different

not the same

interestingly beautiful

you shine unique

a star is born

fear has dulled

your current home

walk into the light

of individuality

that is where you belong

-belonging

I could accept a lower form of love

but I am far too passionate

Everyone has a dark side

everyone has the light

it's the balancing

that drives us crazy

-you are light

You can never be him,
but I don't want you to be
I want a love that embraces me

for who I am
what I have lost
and the importance I place on my
heart

if I show you me
it is important
it is a risk

if I show you me
remember
I have already drowned

and I survived

-survivor

The corridor is dark as I make my
way toward the light
thirteen steps down
and an unforgiving right

I stumble, knees bruised
grabbing walls as I choose
this journey, not far
but infinitely deep
walking past darkness
in order to breathe
the light is there
although I cannot see
through a door waiting to be
opened

by hands of the free

-always there

My hands graze
the Queen Anne's Lace
white tops and fragrant blooms
keep company
along tracks once traveled
sweet summer breezes
bring the scent
of youth gone by
and memories of your eyes
how they searched my lips
for that first kiss

behind corn stalks we hid from
farmers and brothers
just to feel alive
in our small lives
along tracks once traveled
my hands graze
searching for memories

of a once small life

-*small town love*

You were there
rocking in that porch chair
a loose board squeak
pleasing in this dream

we had grown old
enjoying the ease of life
lemonade and the finer things
amidst the sparrow song and the
ravens call
that loose board squeak
quickly became
the most beautiful sound of all

-dreaming

I long for the days
of simple quarrels
where you didn't rinse your milk
glass, or I forgot
to take out the garbage
and when watching my favorite
show caused you to grimace and in
turn a round of tickle torture

I long for the days of simple smiles
when our first pepper plant had
the cutest smallest pepper, but we
smiled so big knowing we grew it
together

I long for the days of knowing
I was loved

and it was the hardest
but easiest thing to be

-loved by you

Your memories

chase me in the darkness

breaking into morning light

as a lonely soul travels

into my shadow you grow

a reminder of once was

collected in the night

and separated by the sun

-infinity

One day
I will wake in arms again
One day
the halls will echo in laughter
One day
I will be asked how my day was
One day
someone will be eating dinner
across from me
One day
all these tears will be wiped
by a kind heart
One day
I will get the embrace of someone
who understands that part of my
heart will always belong

 to someone else

-learning to share

Some hands feel familiar
some feel like passing
some feel like hope
but none have felt like home

-not yet

I saw the ravens
that first spring
circling
scavenging
reminders of death

I saw the ravens
a season next
curious
flying with me
watching the tide

I see the ravens now
and realize
they are not death at all

but adapting to a new sky
just as I have

-adaptations

What we have lost will never be
replaced

what we have lost will survive in
the depths of our souls

what we have lost knows no
bounds of time or distance

but what we have gained is not to
be overlooked or overpowered
a fresh look at this world in a new
light through our grief is
something quite incredible

and something not everyone can
see

-blessings through the pain

At first my sadness
drowned me
in waves coming from all coasts

I had no shore
no lighthouse
just a daily reminder
that I didn't know how to swim

and one day after treading water
far too long I stood up
the storm had left,
and the waves had calmed,
and a smile found its place

I felt guilty then relieved because I
had thought my smile was gone

having buried it with you
but it was there all along letting
sadness take the starring role until
it was ready to shine again

-and now it is the star

I plant seeds in

my hollow places

just in case of rain

memories I hold dear

to tend lovingly

before any pain

I plant seeds in

my hollow places

knowing barren

can be devastating

knowing love can

grow anything

-seeds

C. Churchill

You can replay the tragedy a
million ways

and one day you will accept you
can't stop the universe

I was an island of one
alone with my grief
standing on one foot
allowing the waves to kiss my flesh
while hoping
they would let me drown

I was an island of one until I stood
firmly on two feet and only then
could I allow visitors into my grief

-island of one

You may not be ready to hear it,
but time does help heal
and believe you me I was not ready
to hear it for a long while

I was convinced that I was done,
and I let others take the reins
looking down at me in pity and
sadness

I let myself lose my voice
I let myself lose my happiness
I tried to fit into pants
that were far too small

I tried to fit into an idea
that was handed to me
like hand me downs from someone
who didn't know my size
eventually I taught myself to sew

at first stitching small rips
then piecing together
what scraps I could find

soon I was sewing
more than I was crying
soon I had a beautiful collection
enough to make pants that fit

enough to make any pants I
decided because I was indeed still
growing

-sewing a future

I have sold my soul
for pennies and ink

waiting for true love to
give me another wink

for my words to climb vines
and my verse to beat hearts

I have done this within
a breath and a start

for this pen has no meaning
if it doesn't write

and my voice can't be silenced
if I still fight

so, I spread these words a poet's
truth to never disobey my pen or
my stolen youth
for I have rhymes and I have verse,
but I also have a voice and a truth
that hurts

I will be heard if only under these
wings, burning pages,
I will sing

up in flames the pain will go and
hopefully help another soul as for
me

I begin to fly into the arms where
true love lies

spread your voice over your wings
let it lift you
to better things

-let them hear you

Swallow the flutter
feast the bloom

wildflower born
to race the moon

carry no worries
only wishes and verse

this is the breath
take your first

own the wild
that claws within

embrace the lost
the lust, the sin

claim your voice
it is never too soon

for those born wildflower
to chase the moon

-born wildflower

Through great loss
we either find the floor
or break the ceiling

I have found
I would much rather fly
than crawl

-either way it is bumpy

They may never see
as they hold your leash

opinions matter
how long the lead

keep you safe
keep you here

swearing safety,
they swell your fear

if they would just let you drift
even a little bit

past the comfort
past the line

past all the opinions
of societies crime

maybe you will see
you are meant to be

alive in this world
beautiful and free

there is no task
you cannot face

when you stand your ground
and forget your place

who are they?
to claim your worth

to collar your soul
to erase your birth

you are divine
in every right

to kiss the world
without fright

break the collar
take the lead

wish them well
and begin to breathe

-break free

Shameless, yes, I know
I couldn't help the beasts that roar
in my veins they scream
ripping, sorting
life from pain
they travel well
down trodden paths
reminding me
I have a past
beasts of venom hear me now
I am but a photograph
of what was
not what will be
its time to slit these wrists
and set you free
there is no room for you
in a life that moves forward

-one foot then another

No longer accept being tolerated

when you deserve to be celebrated

Don't let your words
get lost in fear

when you have seen
love as pain

when you can't see a future
because you have seen the shadow
more often than not

don't let it stop your heart
don't let it cloud your voice

that mistake can haunt you forever

-no fear

It took a thousand sunsets
to not feel
your breath in my ear

It will take a thousand more
to not hear your voice

and although these memories are
laced with tears

I dread the day
I can no longer picture

your smile

-memories we hold dear

I have traveled a distance
greater than most
and even though my feet may seem
stuck in mud

I am still moving forward

-distances

racing ravens
chasing pines

finally lost
finally found

among the birches
among the rains

tears shed fiercely
release this pain

for I am wildflower
to be reborn

after the flood
after the storm

-racing ravens

I no longer choose to be a victim

of my own existence

Racing Ravens is not a self-help book and I am not a doctor. Just a widow who knows the loneliness of grief.

Racing Ravens is a collection of my own experiences.

Every tear we lose towards loss is reborn as strength.

I truly believe this statement even though it took me awhile to have faith in it.

Sometimes, when all is lost, we find the greatest places

within ourselves.

Thank you for reading.

About the Author.

C. Churchill is a poet and writer from
Michigan. She currently is residing in
Boston working on future poetry
collections and a novel. She has master's
degree in education and loves helping
students find their creative voice.

On social media

Instagram @cc_writes

Facebook @cc_writes

C. Churchill

Also, by C. Churchill

Petals of the Moon

Wildflower Tea

Coming March 2020

Chasing Pines, the follow up to Racing
Ravens.

Thank you all so very much for your support in his collection.

C. Churchill

C. Churchill

Made in the USA
Monee, IL
02 February 2020

21180179R10056